RiverStream Readers
Great Reading • Real Learning

Ocean Animals

By Emily C. Dawson

RiverStream Readers
Great Reading • Real Learning

Pre1

1

2

Learn to Read

Frequent repetition of sentence structures, high frequency words, and familiar topics provide ample support for brand new readers. Approximately 100 words.

Read Independently

Repetition is mixed with varied sentence structures and 6 to 8 content words per book are introduced with photo labels and picture glossary supports. Approximately 150 words.

Read to Know More

These books feature a higher text load with additional nonfiction features such as more photos, timelines, and text divided into sections. Approximately 250 words.

Accelerated Reader methodology uses Level A instead of Pre1. We have chosen to change it for ease of understanding by potential users.

Amicus Readers hardcover editions published by Amicus. P.O. Box 1329, Mankato, Minnesota 56002 www.amicuspublishing.us

Printed in the United States of America at Corporate Graphics, North Mankato, Minnesota.

Series Editor   Rebecca Glaser
Series Designer   Kia Adams
Photo Researcher   Heather Dreisbach

RiverStream Publishing reprinted by arrangement with Appleseed Editions Ltd.
po
3-2011

Library of Congress Cataloging-in-Publication Data

Dawson, Emily C.
  Ocean animals / by Emily C. Dawson.
    p. cm. – (Amicus readers. Our animal world)
  Includes index.
  Summary: "Compares common ocean animals and how they move through the water. Includes comprehension activity"–Provided by publisher.
  ISBN 978-1-60753-013-8 (library binding)
  1. Marine animals–Juvenile literature. I. Title.
  QL122.2.D386 2011
  591.77–dc22

2010007282

Photo Credits
© Andreas Gradin l Dreamstime.com 16, 21 (m); Christian Musat/123rf, 18–19, 21 (b); Digital Vision, 8, 10, 12, 20 (t, b); Georgette Douwma/Getty Images, cover; Getty Images/Stuart Westmorland, 14, 21 (t); Jeff Hunter/Getty Images, 1; Panoramic Images/Getty Images, 4–5; Photodisc, 6, 20 (m)

1 2 3 4 5 CG 15 14 13 12
RiverStream Publishing—Corporate Graphics, Mankato, MN—112012—1002CGF12

Table of Contents

Many animals live in the ocean. Their body parts help them move.

fin

Fish swim in the ocean.
They use their front fins
to turn.

dorsal fin

8

Sharks swim in the ocean.
They use their dorsal fins
to balance.

flipper

Sea turtles swim in the ocean. They use their front flippers to move forward.

flippers

Dolphins swim in the ocean.
They use their front flippers
to turn and stop.

tail

Whales swim in the ocean.
They use their tails to jump
into the air.

tentacle

Octopuses live in the ocean.
They use their tentacles to
crawl on the ocean floor.

flipper

webbed feet

Penguins swim in the ocean. They flap their flippers to swim. They use their webbed feet to help them steer.

Picture Glossary

dorsal fin
a fin on the back of a
fish that helps it balance

fin
a body part of a fish
that helps it swim, steer,
or balance

flipper
a wide, flat arm of an
ocean animal that helps
it swim

20

tail

a part at the back of an animal's body; Tails of ocean animals help them swim and jump.

tentacle

a long, flexible arm of an octopus or squid that can move, feel, and grab things

webbed feet

feet that have toes joined by a web or fold of skin; Webbed feet help birds swim.

21

What Do You Remember?

1. Trace this chart on a piece of paper.
2. For each animal, place an X in the box that tells which body part it has.

Animal	Fins	Flippers	Tentacles	Webbed Feet
fish				
shark				
turtle				
dolphin				
whale				
octopus				
penguin				

If you don't remember, look back at the words and pictures in the book for the answers.

Ideas for Parents and Teachers

Books 1 through 5 in the RiverStream Readers Level 1 Series give children fascinating facts about animals with lots of reading support. Photo labels and a picture glossary reinforce new vocabulary. The activity page reinforces comprehension and critical thinking. Use the ideas below to help children get even more out of their reading experience.

Before Reading

- Ask the child: What do you know about ocean animals?
- Discuss the photos on the cover and title page. What do these photos show?
- Look at the picture glossary together. Read and discuss the words.

Read the Book

- "Walk" through the book and look at the photos. Let the child ask questions about the photos.
- Read the book to the child, or have him or her read independently.
- Show the child how to read the photo labels and refer to the picture glossary to understand the full meaning as he or she reads.

After Reading

- Use the What Do You Remember? activity on page 22 to help review the text.
- Prompt the child to think more, asking questions such as *What other ocean animals can you think of? What body parts do they have to help them move? Why do you think ocean animals need different body parts than land animals?*

Index

Web Sites

Animal Videos, Photos, Facts—National Geographic Kids
http://kids.nationalgeographic.com/Animals/

Sea World/Busch Gardens—Animals
http://www.seaworld.org

Submarine, Ocean, and Water World
http://www.kbears.com/ocean/index.html

WhaleTimes SeaBed—Whales, Dolphins, Sharks, Penguins, and More
http://www.whaletimes.org/